KU-447-775

Lisa D. Hoff

CHARLESTON

SOUTH CAROLINA

Self-guided Tours in 88 Pictures

CHARLESTON – *Past and Present.*

In April 1670, the frigate *Carolina*, with a group of British settlers, sailed into the harbor formed by the Cooper and Ashley (then called Kiawah) rivers. They built their first settlement on a low bluff overlooking Old Towne Creek.

The expedition, which had been at sea for seven months and had lost two ships, had been financed by the True and Absolute Lord Proprietors of Carolina. The Proprietors were eight politically powerful Englishmen who held a charter from the Crown granting them the lands stretching from North Carolina into Florida and westward to the South Seas.

The settlers included twenty-nine "masters" (men of property) and "free" persons, and sixty-three indentured white servants who had to serve their owners for two to seven years in return for the passage to Carolina, and one or two black slaves. The new settlement soon attracted boatloads of free men and indentured servants from the West Indies and England. Some of the settlers, attracted by the wooded peninsula and the cooler breezes of a site across the Ashley, called White Point or Oyster Point because of the discarded oyster shells left there by the Indians, decided to build there. Charles Town's population increased rapidly, helped by the proprietors who hoped that by advertising Charles Town as being especially healthy and tolerant to all religions they could attract more immigrants who in turn would stimulate the economy and make Charles Town the premier trading harbor with England.

In the mid-1690s, Charles Town was beginning to export rice, which had been imported from Madagascar ten years earlier. This crop was to make some of the planters and merchants the richest men in America. However, the planting, hoeing and harvesting of rice required strong laborers who were immune to malaria and yellow fever. Hundreds of West African slaves arrived in Charles Town each year.

Between 1712 and 1718, Charles Town and its inhabitants were in turn plagued by smallpox and yellow fever, followed by a big hurricane which lasted for twelve hours. When the effects of the hurricane leveled off, the Yamassee Indian War broke out and Indian raiding parties came within a few miles of the walls of Charles Town. When trading after the war started again, pirates seized the ships and plundered their cargo.

In early 1719, the Proprietors disallowed certain import duties passed by the Assembly, prohibited further issuance of money, and ended the policy of granting land to settlers, claiming for themselves the vast lands taken from the Yamassees, and requested the dissolution of the Assembly and a call for new elections. When news arrived in Charles Town that a Spanish armada was being readied to invade Carolina, the Assembly declared itself the new government under His Majesty's protection. Thus ended proprietory government in South Carolina.

The first twenty years of the new Royal Colony were prosperous years. Annually, over 500 oceangoing vessels docked at the eight wharves jutting into the Cooper River.

However, the 1740s brought a slave revolt, nine years of war in Europe, which disrupted the export trade, and the Great Fire of 1740 which destroyed about 300 houses and several wharves and fortifications. After the war, trade resumed with a vengeance. The planters of the lowcountry could not plant enough of the newly introduced crop, indigo, to satisfy the demand for the dye by England's fast-growing textile industry. By the 1760s and early 1770s, the value of Carolina crops soared, and the annual export-import trade exceeded even the

tonnage through New York's port. Well-to-do Charlestonians built grand new houses, the ladies wore the latest London fashions to the theater, to balls and concerts and bought their furniture from Thomas Elfe. Their sons were educated abroad or by private teachers. Three newspapers and the only bookstore and bindery in the South kept the people of Charles Town informed. The port's reputation for being wealthy and unhealthy attracted many physicians, several of whom were Scottish-born and educated, like Alexander Garden, a botanist for whom the gardenia is named, or Lionel Chalmers, who undertook studies of tetanus and meteorology.

On June 28, 1776, while delegates to the Continental Congress in Philadelphia were still debating the issue of separation from the mother country, nine British warships attacked the fort on Sullivan's Island but were forced to retreat. Charles Town was saved. Four months later, the government of Charles Town approved the Declaration of Independence. With the war concentrating in the northeastern states, which interrupted the trade through Boston, New York and Philadelphia, more ships than ever before docked in Charles Town. In 1779, the British, unable to win a decisive battle over Washington's armies and hoping that an invasion of the South would disrupt the trade, sent a massive combined sea and land expedition to Charles Town. After a 42-day siege, America's last open seaport had to surrender. The occupation of Charles Town lasted for two and a half years.

In 1783, the South Carolina legislature dramatically announced the city's new independence from the British Crown by changing the name to Charleston. Three years later they voted over the vigorous opposition of the lowcountry delegation to move the state capital inland to a site that was eventually named Columbia.

Around the turn of the century, a new crop was fast replacing rice and indigo in the export trade. In 1791, South Carolina grew 1.5 million pounds of cotton, a decade later 20 million, and production doubled again within the next ten years. After the Napoleonic Wars the demand for cotton in Europe soared and planters rushed to spend their money on Sea Island mansions and summer homes in the city.

The Medical College of South Carolina opened in 1824 as the South's first school of medicine. A military school, the Citadel, was chartered in 1842. A free public school reformed Charleston's school system into the best in South Carolina. New rail lines connected Charleston with Hamburg, Louisville, Cincinnati, Memphis and Savannah. Charleston became the manufacturing center of South Carolina with numerous rice and grist mills, iron foundries, turpentine distilleries, saw mills, different factories, and a railroad depot and machine shop. The inequality in the distribution of wealth in the city was enormous; some 3 % of the population owned approximately half of all the wealth.

In December 1860, 169 delegates convened in Columbia to vote on secession. The outbreak of smallpox forced the Secession Convention to move to Charleston where they voted 169 : 0 to secede from the Union. Following the formation of the Confederate States of America at Montgomery, Alabama, President Jefferson Davis ordered General Beauregard to take charge of the volatile situation in Charleston. Major Anderson, who had moved his

Federal troops to strategically important Fort Sumter, refused to surrender, and the first shots of the Civil War were fired onto Fort Sumter. For nearly four years Charleston stood defiant in the face of a relentless Federal siege from the sea. When, at last, on the night of February 17, 1865, the Confederate troops finally evacuated their positions, and the city of Charleston fell, it was because Sherman's troops were threatening the state's capital and Charleston's supply lines. Charleston was a city of ruins and desolation.

Economic recovery was slow, but, little by little, the destroyed rail lines and burnt-out sections of the city were rebuilt. Charleston's economy received a boost with the discovery by two scientists at the College of Charleston that phosphate deposits found in the river banks could be used in the manufacturing of fertilizer.

The last quarter of the 19th century saw big changes. The harbor was modernized; the first telephones were installed; new contraptions, called bicycles, and electric trolley cars made the city easily accessible; the crushed shells covering city streets were replaced with flagstones and granite; and finally the city started with its most ambitious and urgent project: replacing the unhealthy privy system with a modern sewage system. Fertilzer factories, saw mills, a cotton factory and sheetmetal works provided jobs, and good profits were made in the crab/shrimp 'industry'.

In 1920, some farsighted Charlestonians launched the first preservation movement. The Society for the Preservation of Old Dwellings, later changed to The Preservation Society of Charleston, saved many landmarks from des-

truction. In 1931, the city of Charleston adopted the first Planning and Zoning Ordinance to protect the historic district.

The transition from an era of segregation to one of equality under the law was a stormy one, but thanks to farsighted black and white leaders, Charleston was the first city in South Carolina to integrate public high schools, municipal facilities, the police force and other city jobs.

In the last twenty years, port activity has expanded rapidly; Charleston has become the number-one containership port on the East Coast. Hundreds of houses have been restored, a new Charleston Museum has been built, and the city has acquired tourist attractions such as Cypress Gardens and Charles Towne Landing. The central business district has been rejuvenated with the construction of Charleston Place, and the Spoleto Festival annually attracts numerous art and music lovers from all over the world. In November 1985, *US News* and *World Report* selected Charleston from seventy-four metropolitan areas as the city "where business is best".

Shortly before midnight on September 21, 1989, Hurricane Hugo, with winds up to 135 mph and pushing a 12- to 17-foot wall of water, roared into Charleston and the surrounding coastal areas. The barrier islands were inundated. Charleston had to be evacuated; trees were uprooted; slate, tin and copper roofs were blown away; chimneys and garden walls collapsed, glass store fronts exploded; and the water pouring through the streets covered everything up to the first floor with mud. Like so often in its 300 years of history, Charleston rallied together the next day and started rebuilding.

Die Geschichte der Stadt Charleston

Im April 1670 segelte das Schiff „Carolina" mit einer Gruppe von Auswanderern aus England kommend in den jetzigen Hafen von Charleston. Ihre erste Siedlung errichteten sie auf einer Anhöhe oberhalb des Ashley-Flusses. Die Expedition, die sieben Monate unterwegs war, war von acht englischen Adeligen finanziert worden. Diese einflussreichen Persönlichkeiten hatten das Gebiet zwischen Nordkarolina und Florida von König Charles II. für die ihm erwiesenen Dienste erhalten.

Zehn Jahre später verlegten die Ansiedler ihre Siedlung auf die Halbinsel zwischen dem Cooper- und dem Ashley-Fluss und nannten sie Charles Town. Die Bevölkerung von Charles Town wuchs schnell, angelockt durch die viel gepriesene Religionsfreiheit. Von Frankreich kamen Hugenotten, von England, den Westindischen Inseln, Schottland und Irland kamen Quäker, Presbyterianer, Baptisten und Juden. Heute noch sind in Charleston über 181 Kirchen, und es wird oft die „Heilige Stadt" genannt. Mitte 1690 begann Charles Town Reis in großen Mengen nach England zu exportieren. Da der Reisanbau sehr arbeitsintensiv war und der Reis nur von Arbeitern angebaut werden konnte, die immun gegen Malaria und Gelbfieber waren, wurden mehr und mehr Sklaven aus Westafrika eingeführt. Als Krieg zwischen England und Frankreich ausbrach, drängten die aristokratischen Landbesitzer darauf, die Stadt zu befestigen. Um 1704 wohnten 3.500 Leute dicht gedrängt innerhalb der Stadtmauern.

Eine ständige Gefahr für die Bewohner Charles Towns waren außer Feuer, Orkanen und Sklavenaufständen die immer wieder auftretenden Seuchen, besonders Pocken und Gelbfieber.

Empört über unzureichenden Schutz, unfaire Gesetze und Gleichgültigkeit von Seiten der adeligen Landbesitzer brachte 1719 die Versammlung (Assembly) von Charles Town eine Petition zur Abschaffung der adeligen Landbesitzer ein und bat um königlichen Schutz. Damit wurde Südkarolina eine königliche Kolonie. Zu diesem Zeitpunkt war Charles Town ein blühender Seehafen. Über 500 Schiffe legten pro Jahr an den acht Kaianlagen entlang des Cooperflusses an, um Luxusartikel, Weine und Sklaven zu entladen und Reis und Indigo für die englischen Märkte zu laden. Charles Town wurde die reichste und viertgrößte Stadt in Kolonialamerika. Die Kaufleute und Pflanzer legten ihr Geld in immer größeren Plantagen, mehr Sklaven und eleganteren Stadthäusern an. Da Malaria im Sommer eine große Gefahr war, verbrachten die meisten Pflanzer mit ihren Familien diese Jahreszeit in der Stadt. Zur Unterhaltung veranstalteten sie Bälle, besuchten Konzerte, Theatervorstellungen oder trafen sich auf den Rennplätzen beim Pferderennen. Die Söhne wurden zur Ausbildung nach England und Schottland geschickt.

Obwohl die Stadt als königliche Kolonie Wohlstand erreichte, führte unfaire Besteuerung zu Widerstand gegen die königliche Oberherrschaft. Während die Delegierten beim Kontinentalen Kongress in Philadelphia 1776 noch darüber debattierten, ob man sich von England trennen sollte, griffen neun englische Kriegsschiffe die Befestigungsanlage auf der Insel Sullivan an. Die Briten wurden zurückgetrieben und das Fort nach seinem Kommandanten Fort Moultrie genannt. Vier Monate später stimmte die Regierung in Charles Town der Unabhängigkeitserklärung zu.

Während sich die Kriegshandlungen im Nordosten Amerikas abspielten, war Charles Town der einzige offene Hafen an der Ostküste. 1779 wurde jedoch Charles Town von den Briten besetzt. Die zweieinhalb Jahre dauernde Besetzung hinterließ tiefe Spuren in der Stadt. Die Stadtteile, die nicht von den Briten beschossen und geplündert worden waren, wurden zum Teil von Feuer zerstört. 1783 wurde die neue Unabhängigkeit dramatisch mit einem neuen Namen für die Stadt angekündigt. Charleston blieb noch drei Jahre die Hauptstadt Südkarolinas. 1786 stimmte die Mehrzahl der gesetzgebenden Versammlung dafür, die Hauptstadt ins Zentrum des Staates zu verlegen, und Columbia wurde gegründet.

Ein neues landwirtschaftliches Produkt verdrängte bald den Reis- und Indigoanbau. 1791 wurden in Südkarolina ca. 1,5 Millionen Pfund Baumwolle angebaut, zehn Jahre später waren es 20 Millionen und 1811 40 Millionen. Für Charleston begann die anmutige Antebellum-Zeit. Neue Eisenbahnlinien stellten die Verbindung mit dem Hinterland her, und Charleston wurde ein Industriezentrum.

Es dauerte jedoch nicht lange und die wirtschaftliche Entwicklung kam zum Stillstand. 1860 trat Südkarolina aus den Vereinigten Staaten aus und bildete mit sieben anderen Südstaaten die Konföderierten Staaten von Amerika. Am 12. April 1861 wurden die ersten Schüsse des Bürgerkrieges von der Konföderierten Armee vom Fort Johnson auf das Fort Sumter abgegeben, das von den Unionsstreitkräften besetzt worden war.

Vier Jahre lang hielt Charleston einem föderalistischen Seeangriff stand. Die konföderierten Streitkräfte gaben erst auf und evakuierten die Stadt, als General Sherman Columbia und somit die Nachschublinie besetzte. Charleston lag in Ruinen. Der Wiederaufbau ging nur langsam vor sich, allerdings erhielt die Wirtschaft durch die Entdeckung, dass Phosphatablagerungen in den Flüssen sich zur Herstellung von Düngemitteln besonders gut eignen, einen Aufschwung. Kurz nach der Jahrhundertwende wurde der Hafen zum bedeutendsten Flottenstützpunkt an der Ostküste ausgebaut. 1920 gründeten einige vorausblickende Bürger die „Gesellschaft zur Erhaltung alter Wohnhäuser", die jetzt unter dem Namen „Preservation Society" bekannt ist. In den letzten zwanzig Jahren ist der Charleston Hafen zum bedeutendsten Containerhafen an der Ostküste herangewachsen. Hunderte von Häusern wurden restauriert, ein neues Museum eröffnet und die Spoletofestspiele locken jeden Sommer Tausende von Musik- und Kunstliebhabern aus aller Welt nach Charleston. Kurz vor Mitternacht am 21. September 1989 fiel Orkan „Hugo" über Charleston und die umliegenden Inseln herein. Bäume wurden entwurzelt, Dächer abgedeckt, Häuser und Kamine stürzten ein und eine 5 Meter hohe Wassermauer, die der Sturm vor sich hertrieb, bedeckte Straßen, Eingänge und Gärten mit braunem Schlamm. Aber wie so oft in seinem 300-jährigen Bestehen ließ sich Charleston mit seinen Bewohnern nicht unterkriegen. Mit Entschlossenheit und Mut fingen sie am nächsten Tag an, die Stadt wiederaufzubauen.

L'Histoire de Charleston

En avril 1670, le vaisseau «Caroline» avec un groupe d'immigrants anglais entra dans le port de Charleston. Les immigrants construirent leur première colonie sur une colline au-dessus de la rivière Ashley. L'expédition, en route pendant sept mois, fut financée par huit Seigneurs anglais. Ces personnages importants avaient reçu du roi Charles II, pour services rendus, le territoire qui s'étend de la Floride à la Caroline du Nord.

Dix ans plus tard ils décidèrent de construire une nouvelle colonie à l'endroit où la rivière Ashley se joint à la rivière Cooper et l'appelerent Charles Town. La population de Charles Town grandit rapidèment, attirée par des assurances de liberté religieuse. De France arrivaient des Huguenots, d'Angleterre, d'Ecosse, d'Ireland et des Antilles venaient, des Anglicans, des Quakers, des Presbytériens, des Baptistes et de Juifs. Aujourd'hui il y a encore plus de 180 églises a Charleston qui est souvent appellée «la Ville Sainte».

En 1695, Charles Town commença à exporter de grandes quantités de riz. Comme la culture du riz exige beaucoup de travail dur sous des conditions malsaines, les planteurs importèrent de plus en plus d'esclaves d'Afrique.

Quand la guerre éclata entre l'Angleterre et la France les propriétaires exigèrent que la ville soit entourée de fortifications. En 1704, 3.500 habitants se serreraient entre ses murailles.

En plus des feux, des ouragans at des révoltes d'esclaves, la population de Charles Town fut constamment menacée d'épidémies, surtout de la variole et de la fièvre jaune.

Dégoute du manque de protection, des lois injustes et de l'insensibilité de la part des propriétaires, l'Assemblé de Charles Town presenta une petition au roi d'abolir le droit de propriété. En 1720 la Caroline du Sud devint une colonie royale.

Charles Town était un port fleurissant. Chaque année plus de 500 navires entraient dans le port pour décharger des articles de luxe, des vins et des esclaves et pour embarquer du riz et de l'indigo destinés aux marchés anglais. Charles Town devint la ville la plus riche d'Amérique.

Les marchands et les planteurs investirent dans des plantations de plus en plus grandes, ce qui exigea l'importation accélérée d'esclaves. Plus que la moitié de la population de Charles Town fut des esclaves. Comme la malaria fut prévalente, la plupart de planteurs et leurs familles passèrent, l'été dans leurs maisons de ville. Pour se divertir, ils allaient aux bals, aux concerts, au théâtre et au courses de chevaux. Les fils étaient éduqués en Angleterre ou en Ecosse, les filles passaient une année de pensionnat à Charleston ou à Baltimore.

Des taxations injustes amenaient les colonies américaines à se révolter contre le Roi et le Parlement anglais. Pendant que les délégués au Congrès Continental à Philadelphie discutaient de la séparation avec l'Angleterre, neuf navires de guerre anglais attaquèrent l'île Sullivan a l'entrée du port de Charles Town. Apres la première victoire de la Révolution américaine le fort fut nommé Fort Moultrie d'après son commandant. Quatre mois après, les délégués, dont quatre étaient de Charles Town, signerent la Déclaration d'Indépendance. Pendant la Révolution Charles Town fut le seul port des États-Unis qui resta ouvert. En 1776, l'armée anglais occupa Charles Town. Après l'occupation, qui dura deux ans et demi la moitie de Charles Town fut détruite.

En 1783, Charles Town devint Charleston. Trois ans plus tard la législature décida d'établir une nouvelle capitale, Columbia, au centre de Caroline du Sud.

Un nouveau produit commençait à prendre la place du riz et de l'indigo. En 1781, la Caroline plantait à peu près 1,5 millions livres de coton, dix ans plus tard c'était 20 millions et en 1811 40 millions. Pour Charleston commença la période Antebellum avec ses maisons élégantes. Des chemins de fer liaient Charleston à d'autre villes, et elle devenait bientôt le centre industriel du sud.

Malheureusement ce boom ne dura pas longtemps. En 1860, la Caroline du Sud, à cause de la question de l'esclavage, sortit de l'union des États-Unis et forma avec les sept états du Sud les Etats Confédérés d'Amérique. Le 12 avril 1861,1'armée confédérée tirait le premier coup de feu de la guerre civile sur les troupes unionistes à Fort Sumter. Pendant, quatre ans Charleston résista aux attaques maritimes de la marine fédéraliste. A la fin de la guerre Charleston se retrouva en ruines.

La reconstruction fut longue et dure. La demande du coton sur le marchés europeens diminuait, et seule la découverte que les dépots de phosphate dans les rivières autour de Charleston produisaient des fertilisants sauva l'économie de Charleston.

En 1920, quelques Charlestoniens prévoyants créèrent la «Société pour Préserver les Vielles Maisons». Depuis lors la Société de Préservation a sauvé des centaines de maisons de la destruction.

Aujourd'hui Charleston attire des visiteurs du monde entier avec ses belles maisons, son climat tempéré et surtout le Festival de Spoleto. Le 21 septembre 1989, vers minuit l'ouragan «Hugo» se lançait sur Charleston et les îles voisines. Il arracha des arbres et des toits, renversa des murs et des cheminées et couvra les rues et les premiers étages des maisons d'eau sale. Mais le lendemain, comme à plusieurs reprises dans ses 300 ans d'existence, Charleston reprit ses forces et recommença sa reconstruction.

Photo Credit:

Charleston Museum of Art (page 47)
Charleston Post Card Company (page 7)
Gibbes Museum (page 34)
Anne-Christine Hoff (pages 9, 28, 42, 51)
Richard Lubrant (pages 4b, 60, 61)
John W. Meffert (pages 38, 52)
Stills Photo (page 6)
The Abby Aldrich Rockefeller Folk Art Center (page 32)

Maps and Artworks:

Elisabeth Hoff

The first permanent English settlement in the Province of Carolina was established in 1670 at Charles Towne Landing across the Ashley River. Ten years later Charles Town was moved to its present location. The city which withstood attacks by the French, Spanish, Indians and pirates was protected by earthen walls and a moat. The entrance from the landward side was over a draw bridge at the corner of Broad Street and Meeting Street.

City Hall was designed by Charlestonian, Gabriel Manigault, a wealthy rice planter, powerful Federalist and accomplished amateur architect, as a branch office of the First Bank of the United States. The city's seal was adopted in 1783 and can be seen on the pediment. This junction is called the "Four Corners of Law" with City Hall (1801), St. Michael's Church (1761), Federal Courthouse and Charleston Courthouse (1792) representing the "Law."

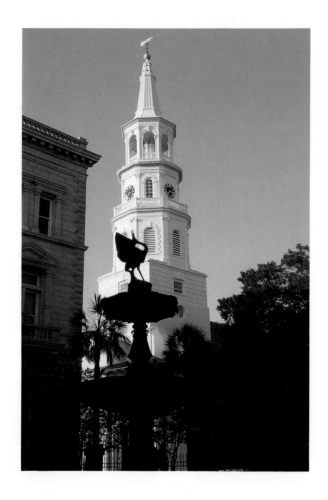

St. Michael's Episcopal Church, considered one of the finest Colonial churches, was completed in 1761. The bells have been cast in England in 1764. They have crossed the Atlantic five times. After the Revolution, they were sent back as spoils of war. A London merchant bought them and sent them back. During the Civil War, they were sent to Columbia for safekeeping and melted during the burning. The metal was then shipped back to England for recasting.

Nathaniel Russel House (51 Meeting Street), built 1808, is recognized as one of America's finest example of Neoclassical domestic architecture. Each floor contains only three rooms, one square, one rectangular and one oval. A free-flying staircase connects the three floors. Nathaniel Russel was a prominent merchant from New England who came to Charleston as a young man and quickly amassed a fortune.

Calhoun Mansion (16 Meeting Street), built 1876, with its 25 rooms is considered to be the largest single family residence in the city. The interior of this building boasts original walnut and oak woodwork and beautiful gas chandeliers. The house is named in honor of one of its former owners, Patrick Calhoun, a grandson of John C. Calhoun, the South Carolina legislator, secretary of war, and vice-president.

South Battery. The mansions of the Battery, the peninsula's southernmost tip, were built after 1820 and are newer than their neighbors inland. Before the Battery was a fashionable address, it was a marsh. On April 11, 1861, Charlestonians rushed to the Battery to watch and cheer the bombardment of Fort Sumter. The fall of the fort two days later signified the beginning of the Civil War.

The Battery was named White Pointe by the first settlers for the discarded oyster shells the Indians hat left there. In 1718, pirates who had long terrorized merchant ships up and down the coast boldly entered the harbor and plundered several ships. Angry merchants outfitted two warships and caught the notorious pirate, Stede Bonnet. He and his crew were hanged at White Pointe and buried below the high-water mark off the point.

Battery

East Battery. The story goes that the Ashley and the Cooper rivers meet at Charleston to form the Atlantic Ocean. Notice that the piazzas of the houses on East Battery do not face the Cooper River. The Charleston single house is turned in the direction from which the afternoon breezes blow in from the Atlantic – like "a ship at full sail trimmed to catch the wind."

The Louis de Saussure House (1 E Battery) was built in 1838 in late Greek-Revival style. The cast-iron balconies were added in the 1880s. The house occupies what is considered the most desirable location in the city with commanding views of both the Ashley River and the Cooper River, the entire harbor and the sea beyond. The house passed through several owners before becoming three condominiums.

The John Ravenel House (5 E Battery) was constructed circa 1848 on one of the reclaimed marshland lots sold by the city. In this house Dr. John St. Julien Ravenel, a doctor, planter and scientist, designed a 50-foot-long, cigar-shaped torpedo boat, the *"Little David"*, which during the Civil War, attacked and damaged what was then the largest ironclad frigate in the world.

The Edmonston-Alston House (21 E Battery). The house was built in 1825 by Charles Edmonston, a Scottish-born merchant. Economic reversals during the Panic of 1837 forced him to sell the house to Charles Alston, member of a well established low-country rice-planting dynasty. The house, after having been modified in the fashionable Greek-Revival style, became the Alston city residence and is still in the family.

13

East drawing room of the Edmonston-Alston House. The drawing rooms are located on the second floor where piazza doors could be thrown open to catch the breeze. The family bedrooms occupied the third floor. Business visitors were received on the first floor. Alston family furniture, silver, books and paintings decorate the high-ceilinged rooms. The first two floors are open to the public.

The Porcher-Simonds House (25 E Battery) was built by a cotton broker a few years before the Civil War. The double-tiered semicircular front piazza was added later. All of the side piazzas were enclosed during the Second World War, when the house was used by the U. S. Office of Naval Intelligence. A young John F. Kennedy occupied one of the offices. The house was converted into three condominiums in 1983.

Stoll's Alley. This early Charleston alley, originally named for the blacksmith, Justinus Stoll, contains several pre-Revolutionary brick dwellings. 7 Stoll's Alley, built and inhabited by Stoll in 1745, initially consisted of two rooms. Charleston's alleys usually date from the mid-eighteenth century. They were thoroughfares that housed Irish immigrants and free African American tradesmen.

Tradd Street illustrates early eighteenth-century construction in the densely populated walled city. Most of the structures built in this area during this time are only two stories with one or two rooms per story. Small passages lead to work yards in the rear. Lots with street frontage were at such a premium that buildings covered the whole lot, unlike later Charleston houses which included a side yard and piazzas.

Heyward-Washington House (87 Church Street). This brick double house with a central hall and two rooms on each side was the home of Thomas Heyward, a signer of the Declaration of Independence. It was built in 1772. The house is furnished with Charleston-made furniture, including the Holmes bookcase, considered to be the finest example of American-made furniture in existence. The Heyward House was the first house museum in Charleston.

The kitchen with the slave quarters above and the other outbuildings of the Heyward-Washington House were constructed in 1740. Thomas Heyward who preferred to live on his plantation to living in the city rented the house to the city as lodging for President George Washington during his week-long stay in Charleston in 1791. The garden is planted with flowers which were known in South Carolina at the time of the presidential visit.

19

Catfish Row (89-91 Church Street). This building (built ca. 1783) achieved fame as the residence of Porgy, the crippled beggar in Gershwin's opera *Porgy and Bess*. When Dubose Heyward wrote the novel *Porgy* he described "Goat-Cart-Sammy", a real-life person, who would ride on a goat-drawn cart up and down Church Street while holding out his cup.

These three houses (90, 92 and 94 Church Street), built in 1759, 1760 and 1805, have been called by architectural historians "three variations of the Charleston single house." Charleston's most elegant houses were built around that time when a booming rice and indigo export made the city the fourth largest in British North America. Number 94 was the town home of Governor Joseph Alston and his famous and beautiful wife Theodosia, daughter of Aaron Burr.

Rainbow Row (79-107 E Bay Street). These houses were originally on the waterfront and served as residences and as offices for prosperous merchants. The ground floors were used by factors as counting rooms and stores. As the docks silted, the wharves were moved to other locations on the Cooper River where the waterlevel was higher.

Waterfront Park.

Old Exchange Building & Provost Dungeon (122 E Bay Street). The completion in 1771 of this elegant Georgian-style Exchange marked the beginning of Charleston's golden era as the wealthiest city in British North America. During the American Revolution while the British occupied Charleston, the basement became the Provost Dungeon where suspected rebels were incarcerated. The Old Exchange & Provost Dungeon are operated as a museum.

View of Broad Street.

The Pink House (17 Chalmers Street), built in 1712 of pinkish Bermuda stone, is the sole surviving colonial alehouse that lined Chalmers Alley, a bawdy and rowdy tavern district. In 1773, Charleston, a city of some 10,000 people, had over a hundred "tippling houses," as public taverns for sailors and laborers were known, half of which were licensed to women. The more respectable taverns on Church and Tradd streets served wine or molasses and parsimmons beer.

Dock Street Theatre (136 Church Street) was built inside the shell of the once elegant "Planters' Hotel." The original Dock Street Theatre was built in 1736 near the present structure. Many upcountry planters brought their families and servants to Charleston for several weeks in February to take in the social season and attend the horse races. The hotel is said to be the birthplace of planters' punch.

French Huguenot Church (132 Church Street). Huguenot refugees from France fleeing religious persecution after Louis XIV revoked the Edict of Nantes which had guaranteed their right of religious freedom established this congregation in 1687. This church, built in 1844, was the first Gothic-Revival building in Charleston and is one of the few Huguenot churches still in existance in America today. The organ is the original Henry Erben and was installed in 1847.

St. Philip's Episcopal Church (146 Church Street). Anglicans built Charleston's first church in 1683 at the corner of Meeting and Broad streets. In 1722, St. Philip's was moved to this site. After it burned down in 1835, reconstruction was started on the present church which is regarded by many as the most beautiful in the city. George Washington worshiped in this church, Edward Rutledge, signer of the Declaration of Independence, and John Calhoun are buried in the churchyard.

Old Powder Magazine (21 Cumberland Street). The Powder Magazine, built 1713, is the oldest secular public building in South Carolina and the only one dating from the time of Proprietary rule. In the nineteenth century, the structure was used as a livery stable, printing shop and as a private wine cellar to the Manigault family. In 1993, the Historic Charleston Foundation restored the site and opened it to the public.

City Market

Market Hall (188 Meeting Street). Charles Hamilton's *Charleston Square* shows the market area in 1865. Market Hall and the public market sheds behind the hall were the center of Charleston's nineteenth-century commercial district. The land was given to the city in 1788 by Charles Cotesworth Pinckney with the clause, which continues to this day, that the land would revert to the Pinckney family if the city ceases to use it as a public market.

Circular Congregational Church (150 Meeting Street). The Independent or Congregational Church has met at this location since its establishment in 1681. The first congregation was made up by Huguenots, Scottish and Irish Presbyterians and Congregationalists from New England. The first building was called the White Meeting House, hence Meeting Street. This is the fourth church (built 1892) on this site. The churchyard has been in use since 1681.

Gibbes Museum of Art (135 Meeting Street). The Gibbes collection consists of over 7,000 objects ranging from paintings, prints and drawings to miniature rooms and the country's premiere collection of miniature portraits.

Hibernian Society Hall (105 Meeting Street). The Hibernian Society was established in 1801 to provide aid to Irish immigrants and their families. The hall is the site of numerous social functions, including the annual St. Patrick's Day banquet and the ball of the St. Cecilia Society. The stone on the portico was brought from Northern Ireland in 1851, it is from the Giant's Causeway. The elaborate wrought-iron gate features the outline of an Irish harp.

35

Fireproof Building (100 Meeting Street). The Public Records Office was designed by Robert Mills in 1822. Mills was born in Charleston in 1781. After his apprenticeship with James Hoban, architect of the White House, Mills was hired by Thomas Jefferson to make drawings of designs for Monticello. In 1803, he entered the architectural office of Benjamin H. Latrobe, Surveyor of Public Buildings. This building was the first fireproof building in America.

Ornamental ironwork is a Charleston tradition.

The poinsettia was named for Charlestonian Joel Poinsett.

The art of lowcountry basket making was brought from West Africa.

Dr. John Lining House (106 Broad Street). The John Lining House is the oldest frame structure in Charleston, it was built before 1715. Dr. John Lining recorded America's first scientific weather observations at his home in 1737. His findings were published by the Royal Society of London.

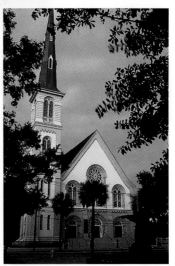

Nicknamed the "Holy City", Charleston has 181 churches.

Colonel John Stuart House (106 Tradd Street). This lavishly constructed house was built in 1767 by John Stuart, a Scotsman, who became superintendent of Indian affairs for the southern colonies of Virginia, North Carolina, South Carolina and Georgia. He had to flee Charleston, and his vast properties were confiscated, when rumors circulated that, as his majesty's agent, he had tried to incite the Catawba and Cherokee Indians against the colonials.

Sword Gate (32 Legare Street) and Pineapple Gate (14 Legare Street). From 1750 onward, with ever greater profits from rice and indigo, Charleston prospered and the construction of bigger houses caused the city to spill beyond the boundaries of the old walled city. The wrought-iron gates have an elaborate sword and spear design and were made by the iron worker, Christopher Werner. The stone pineapples are said to have been carved in Italy.

The South Carolina Aquarium (100 Aquarium Wharf). An exhibition path leads visitors through the five major regions of the Southeast Appalachian Watershed: the Blue Ridge Mountains, the Piedmont, the Coastal Plains, the Coast and the open Ocean. The aquarium extends out over the Charleston Harbor with panoramic views of sailing ships, Fort Sumter and the birds and fish that live in South Carolina's salt marshes and estuaries.

The Aiken-Rhett House (48 Elizabeth Street) was built by a Charleston merchant in 1818. After John Robinson lost five ships in one year, the mansion was sold to William Aiken, Jr., governor of South Carolina and successful businessman and rice planter. This "urban plantation" has survived virtually unaltered since 1858. The house and the original outbuildings have remained in the family till 1975. The house is owned by the Historic Charleston Foundation.

Joseph Manigault House (350 Meeting Street). About 1803, gentleman-architect, Gabriel Manigault, designed this Adam-style house for his brother Joseph. The house with its second-floor drawing room and withdrawing room, and outstanding collection of American, English and French furnishings captures the lifestyle of the wealthy rice-planting family. The Garden Club of Charleston restored the garden according to a 1820 watercolor by Charlotte Manigault.

The Charleston Museum (360 Meeting Street), founded in 1773, is America's first museum. In front of the museum is a replica of the Confederate Submarine *Hunley* which sank the Union warship, *Housatonic*, in the first successful submarine attack in the Charleston Harbor in 1864. Unfortunately, the sub and its crew of nine sank before it returned to port. In 2000, the *Hunley* was carefully raised and is being examined at the Warren Lasch Conservation Center.

Charles Town's colonial houses were built in a distinct architectural style derived from England, Barbados and the West Indies. All houses on this page are pre-Revolutionary. The typical Charleston house was called a "single house" because it was only one room wide. The single house was usually three stories high with two rooms on each floor. A public entrance led from the street to the shop or office in the front of the house.

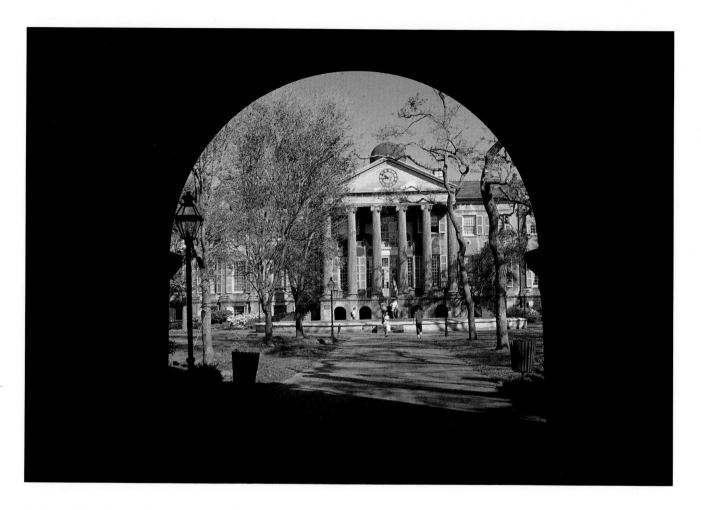

College of Charleston (66 George Street). Founded in 1770 and chartered in 1785, the College of Charleston is the oldest institution of higher learning in South Carolina, and the 13th oldest in America. The Harrison Randolph Hall was designed by William Strickland of Philadelphia, a student of Benjamin Latrobe, one of the architects of the U.S.Capitol.

The Citadel (171 Moultrie Street) was founded in 1842 as the South Carolina Military Academy. The heavily armed, highly visible cadets who drilled on the parade ground in front of the institution were to uphold public order and to receive a "broad and practical education". Today the Citadel is also open to women. The Citadel Museum is located on the campus. The dress parade is Friday afternoons during the college year.

Fort Sumter. This man-made island fort at the entrance of Charleston Harbor was one of four solitary Union forts in the South. On April 12, 1861, General P.G.T. Beauregard, in command at Charleston, ordered the bombardment of the fort which lasted for 34 hours. With his ammunition nearly gone, his provisions exhausted and the fort on fire, the Federal commander, Major Robert Anderson, surrendered. This was the beginning of the Civil War.

Charleston Harbor.

Patriots Point Naval and Maritime Museum. The aircraft carrier *Yorktown* whose planes inflicted heavy damage in the Pacific during WWII, is the flagship of the Patriots Point fleet. The submarine *Clamogore* operated in the Atlantic and the Mediterranean. The destroyer *Laffey* participated in the D-day landings of the Allied troops in Normandy. The Coast Guard cutter *Ingham* took part in 31 WWII convoys, six Pacific patrols and three Vietnam tours.

Fort Moultrie. This original palmetto log fort was only half completed when attacked by the British fleet on June 28, 1776. Colonel William Moultrie's men repelled the assault in one of the first decisive victories of the Revolution. Almost a century later, the Confederate-held fort with about 40 guns and 500 men withstood Federal bombardments during a 20-months siege. 1n 1947, Fort Moultrie was deactivated.

Boone Hall Plantation. Major John Boone, who arrived from England in 1681, received the land as a grant from the Lords Proprietors. Boone Hall which covered more than 17,000 acres was a cotton plantation. Bordering the avenue of oaks are nine original slave cabins. The house servants and plantation's skilled craftsmen were housed in these cabins. The present mansion, built in 1935, was one of the plantation homes in the TV film "North and South."

Charles Pinckney National Historic Site. Snee Farm was purchased by Charles Pinckney's father in 1754. Charles Pinckney, one of the signers of the Constitution, preferred Snee Farm to his other six plantations and stayed here often. No structures remain from the time the Pinckneys lived here. The present house, built in 1820, is a good example of a tidewater cottage. It contains exhibits on Charles Pickney, his family, his political career and his time.

Charles Towne Landing - 1670. In April 1670, some 93 colonists settled on this neck of land. The Proprietors had promised all free settlers over sixteen years of age 150 acres of land and an additional 100 acres for every able-bodied man servant they brought with them. Of the 93 settlers 29 were masters and free people, the rest were indentured servants. A guided tram tour takes visitors through the original fortification and Settler's Life Area.

Drayton Hall was built between 1738 and 1742 for John Drayton, the heir of some twenty rice, indigo and cotton plantations in Carolina, Georgia and Canada. Seven generations of the Drayton family lived at Drayton Hall. In 1974, it was sold to the National Trust for Historic Preservation. Drayton Hall has often been called the first true Palladian house in America. Scenic trails let visitors explore the banks of the Ashley River and the surrounding marshland.

Magnolia Plantation and Gardens has been the ancestral home of the Drayton family for over 300 years. The original plantation house was burned by Federal troops during the Civil War. The gardens, which were started in 1830, have an extensive collection of plants and trees. Do not miss the Audubon Swamp Garden and the Biblical Garden, as well as the petting zoo, a mini horse ranch and miles of trails and boardwalks.

Middleton Place. The house and plantation were part of Mary Williams's dowry when she married Henry Middleton in 1741. Henry started the gardens the same year. The present house was added in 1755 as a gentlemen's guest wing. The house became the family residence after the plantation was burned during the Civil War. Some of the first camellias and azaleas to be planted in American gardens were planted at Middleton Place in 1786.

Cypress Gardens was originally part of Dean Hall Plantation. In 1909, Benjamin Kittredge purchased Dean Hall and converted the destroyed rice fields, dikes and swamp into a year-round-blooming swamp garden. In the spring, the 163-acre garden blazes with azaleas, camellias, dogwoods, wisterias and wildflowers. A working rice field explains how rice was grown. Explore Cypress Gardens either from flat-bottom boats or by walking the nature trails.

Old Santee Canal State Park is the site of America's first canal which began operating in 1800. It was considered a marvel of engineering. Before the Santee Canal connected the Santee River with the Cooper River, crops from the fertile uplands were shipped overland by wagon or floated down the Santee River into the Atlantic and then rowed along the coast to Charleston. Visitors will find miles of boardwalks and trails. Canoes are available for exploring.

Mepkin Abbey. The American patriot, Henry Laurens, purchased Mepkin (which means *serene and lovely* in Native American) in 1762. Laurens was captured by the British as he traveled to France to negotiate military aid and was held in the Tower of London till the end of the American Revolution. He was exchanged for Lord Cornwallis. In 1936, Mepkin was purchased by Henry and Clare Booth Luce, the publishers of Life Magazine, who gave it to the Cistercian order.

The Angel Oak is a live oak (Quercus virginiana), a native tree species found throughout the lowcountry. The age of the Angel Oak has long been reported to be in excess of 1,400 years but this has never been scientifically established. However, only in the very oldest specimens are the limbs resting on the ground. The tree was named for Justis Angel, one of the owners of the property. The City of Charleston now owns Angel Oak Park.

Index Charleston

Charleston Heritage Passport is a combination ticket which includes the following sites: Nathaniel Russell House, Edmonston-Alston House, Aiken-Rhett House, Gibbes Museum of Art, Drayton Hall, Middleton Place (stable and gardens).

Historic Charleston

Tour 1 is a walking tour which starts at the corner of Broad and Meeting Street, south on Meeting Street to South Battery, then East Battery to Stoll's Alley to Church Street, north on Church Street to Market Street, south on Meeting Street to point of departure.

Page (numbers on maps correspond to page numbers)

30   **Old Powder Magazine,** 79 Cumberland Street, Tel.: 843-805-6730
Hours: Mon. - Sat. 10 - 5, Sun. 2 - 5
Admission: Yes (combination ticket with Nathaniel Russel House & Aiken-Rhett House)

34   **Gibbes Museum of Art,** 135 Meeting Street, Tel.: 843-722-2706
Hours: Tue. - Sat. 10 - 5, Sun. 1 - 5
Admission: Yes

Aquarium, Aiken-Rhett House, Joseph Manigault House, Charleston Museum

Tour 2 starts with the South Carolina Aquarium and the Charleston Harbor then west on Calhoun Street, north on Elizabeth Street and west on John Street to Meeting Street. Also see the Charleston Visitors Center across from the Charleston Museum.

44   **South Carolina Aquarium,** 100 Aquarium Wharf (parking garage on Calhoun Street.)
DASH shuttle service is available from the Charleston Visitor Center.
Tel.: 843-720-1990, www.scaquarium.org
Hours: Daily 9 - 5 (June 15 till August 15 open from 9 to 6)
Admission: Yes

45   **Aiken-Rhett House,** 48 Elizabeth Street, Tel. 843-723-1159
Hours: Mon. - Sat. 10 - 5, Sun. 2 - 5 (last tour 4:30)
Admission: Yes (combination ticket with Nathaniel Russell House & Old Powder Magazine)

46   **Joseph Manigault House,** 350 Meeting Street, Tel.: 843-722-2996
Hours: Mon. - Sat. 10 - 5, Sun. 1 - 5
Admission: Yes (combination ticket with Heyward-Washington House & Charleston Museum)

47   **Charleston Museum,** 360 Meeting Street, Tel.: 843-722-2996
Hours: Mon. - Sat. 10 - 5, Sun. 1 - 5
Admission: Yes (combination ticket with Heyward-Washington House & Manigault House)

            The Karpeles Manuscript Library Museums (not shown), 68 Spring Street
Tel.: 843-853-4651, www.karpeles.com
Hours: Tue. - Sat. 11 - 4
Admission: Free

Citadel, Forts and Naval Museum

50   **Citadel Museum,** 171 Moultrie Street, Tel.: 843-953-6846
Hours: Sun. - Fri. 2 - 5, Sat. 12 - 5
Admission: Free
Dress parade Fridays at 3:45 during school year.

51   **Fort Sumter National Monument,** Charleston Harbor
National Park Service Fort Sumter: 843-883-3123
Park Hours: Daily 10 - 6 (September to November, March to April 10 - 5)
Tour boats leave daily for a 2-hour tour from City Marina on Lockwood Dr. (9:30, 12:00, 2:30) or from Patriots Point Maritime Museum (10:45, 1:30, 4:00)
Fort Sumter Tours, Inc., P. O. Box 59, Charleston, SC 29402, Tel.: 843-722-1691

53   **Patriots Point Naval & Maritime Museum,** 40 Patriots Point Road, Mount Pleasant,
Tel.: 843-884-2727
Hours: Daily 9 - 7:30 (October through March 9 - 6:30)
Admission: Yes

54   **Fort Moultrie,** Fort Sumter National Monument, 1214 Middle Street, Sullivans Island
Tel.: 843-883-3123
Hours: Daily 9 - 5 (Summer 9 - 6)
Admission to Visitors Center: Free (nominal user fee for entrance to fort)

Plantations in Mount Pleasant

55   **Boone Hall Plantation,** Long Point Road off Highway 17 N, Mount Pleasant
Tel.: 843-884-4371
Hours: Mon. - Sat. 8:30 - 6:30, Sun. 1 - 5 (October through March 9 - 5, Sun. 1 - 4)
Admission: Yes

56   **Charles Pinckney National Historic Site,** 1254 Long Point Road, Mount Pleasant (off Hwy 17N),
Tel.: 843-881-5516 or 843-883-3123
Hours: Daily 9 - 5 (Summer 9 - 6)
Admission: Free

Charles Towne Landing and Plantations on the Ashley River

57   **Charles Towne Landing - 1670,** 1500 Old Town Road (Hwy 61, right on Hwy 171)
Tel.: 843-852-4200
Hours: Daily 8:30 - 5 (Summer 8:30 - 6)
Admission: Yes

58   **Drayton Hall, National Trust,** 3380 Ashley River Road (Hwy 61), Tel.: 888-349-0588 (Museum Shop: 843-769-2610), www.draytonhall.org
Hours: Daily 10 - 4 (November to February 10 - 3)
Admission: Yes

59   **Magnolia Plantation and Gardens,** Ashley River Road (Hwy 61), Tel.: 843-571-1266
Hours: Daily 8 - 5:30
Admission: Yes

60   **Middleton Place,** 4300 Ashley River Road (Hwy 61), Tel.: 843-556-6020, www.middletonplace.org
Hours: Daily 9 - 5
Admission: Yes (separate admission for house and gardens)

Moncks Corner and Cooper River

61   **Cypress Gardens,** 3030 Cypress Gardens Road, Moncks Corner, SC 29461
Tel.: 843-553-0515
Hours: Daily 9 - 5
Admission: Yes

62   **Old Santee Canal State Park,** 900 Stony Landing Road, Moncks Corner, SC 29461
Tel.: 843-899-5200
Hours: Daily 9 - 5 (Summer 9 - 6)
Admission: Free

63   **Mepkin Abbey,** 1098 Dr. Evans Road, Moncks Corner, SC 29461 (6 miles from SC 402)
Tel.: 843-761-8509
Hours: Daily 9 - 4:30. Midday Prayer, a ten-minute chanted service, is at noon.
Admission: Free

Johns Island and Wadmalaw Island

64   **Angel Oak Park,** 3688 Angel Oak Rd., Johns Island, SC 29455 (Hwy 17 S then Hwy 171/Main Road), Tel.: 843-559-3496
Hours: Mon. - Sat. 9 - 5, Sun. 1 - 5
Admission: Free

Charleston Tea Plantation (not shown), 6617 Maybank Hwy, Madwalaw Island, SC 29487 (from Hwy 17 S take Hwy 171/Main Rd. then Maybank Hwy.) This is the only tea plantation in the U.S.
Tel.: 843-559-0383
Hours: Please call for hours of operation
Admission: Yes for guided tours

Calendar of Annual Events

Charleston Convention & Visitors Center, 81 Mary Street, Charleston, SC 29402, Tel.: 843-853-8000, www.charlestoncvb.com.

Historic Charleston Foundation, 108 Meeting Street, Charleston, SC 29401, Tel.: 843-724-8484, www.historiccharleston.org.

The Preservation Society of Charleston, 147 King Street, Charleston, SC 29401, Tel.: 843-722-4630.

For current events also visit www.charlestoncitypaper.com.

January:	Annual Holiday Festival of Lights, Lowcountry Oyster Festival
January - March:	Plantation Days at Middleton Place
February:	Camellia Walks at Middleton Place
April:	Cooper River Bridge Run (check date)
May:	Lowcountry Strawberry Festival
May & June:	Spoleto Festival and Piccolo Spoleto Festival
September & October:	Annual Fall Candlelight Tours of Homes, MOJA African American Arts Festival
October:	Charleston Garden Show, The Autumn Family Fest
December:	Plantation Christmas, Annual Holiday Festival of Lights

BOOKS BY CITIES IN COLOR, INC.

SAVANNAH IN 88 PICTURES
GEORGIA IN 88 PICTURES
COLUMBIA, SC, IN 88 PICTURES
NEW ORLEANS IN 88 PICTURES
SANTA FE IN 88 PICTURES
ST. AUGUSTINE IN 88 PICTURES
SAN ANTONIO IN 88 PICTURES

RIO DE JANEIRO, BRAZIL
BRASILIA, BRAZIL

VIENNA, AUSTRIA
INNSBRUCK, AUSTRIA
SALZBURG, AUSTRIA

CITIES IN COLOR, INC
12 BRAEMORE DRIVE, NW
ATLANTA GA 30328-4845
TEL.: 404-255-1054, FAX: 404-252-7218
E-MAIL: GMHOFF@AOL.COM
www.citiesincolor.com

© CITIESINCOLOR, INC.